FAIRIES

PICTURE WINDOW BOOKS
a capstone imprint

Mythical Creatures is published by
Picture Window Books, an imprint of Capstone.
1710 Roe Crest Drive
North Mankato, Minnesota 56003
capstonepub.com

Copyright © 2022 by Capstone. All rights reserved. No part of this publication may be reproduced in whole or in part, or stored in a retrieval system, or transmitted in any form or by any means, electronic, mechanical, photocopying, recording, or otherwise, without written permission of the publisher.

Library of Congress Cataloging-in-Publication Data
Names: Subramaniam, Suma, author. | Bustamante, Martín (Illustrator), illustrator.
Title: Fairies / Suma Subramaniam; illustrated by Martín Bustamante.
Description: North Mankato, Minnesota: Picture Window Books, [2022] | Series: Mythical creatures | Includes bibliographical references. | Audience: Ages 5–7 | Audience: Grades K–1 | Summary: "Gaze at that sparkling light, dancing in the sky! It's a fairy, one of nature's greatest treasures. Have you ever wondered where fairies live? What she eats and how she uses her magic? Wonder no more! Striking illustrations and matter-of-fact text take you on a magical journey to learn all about fairies."— Provided by publisher.
Identifiers: LCCN 2021006154 (print) | LCCN 2021006155 (ebook) | ISBN 9781663909626 (hardcover) | ISBN 9781663909596 (ebook pdf) | ISBN 9781663909619 (kindle edition)
Subjects: LCSH: Fairies—Juvenile literature.
Classification: LCC GR549 .S83 2022 (print) | LCC GR549 (ebook) | DDC 398.21—dc23
LC record available at https://lccn.loc.gov/2021006154
LC ebook record available at https://lccn.loc.gov/2021006155

Editor: Julie Gassman
Designer: Hilary Wacholz

All internet sites appearing in back matter were available and accurate when this book was sent to press.

Printed and bound in the USA. 004270

FAIRIES

by Suma Subramaniam

illustrated by Martín Bustamante

It's a warm day in the village. Everyone is going about their work. Everything is normal. But then you see a faint light. You follow it and notice wings.

Before you can catch a glimpse, it disappears in a flash. You wonder what it could be. A bird? A dragonfly?

Or maybe it is something more magical . . . a fairy, perhaps?

WHAT IS A FAIRY?

A fairy is a mythical creature who looks like a human, often with wings. The word fairy comes from the Latin word *fata*, or spirit. "Faerie" is also an old French spelling. Fairies can be both female and male. Some people say that fairies don't exist. But fairies have lived with us in stories for a long time.

FAIRY BEHAVIOR

Because fairies are magical, they have endless abilities. They can fly across the sky. They can tumble deep down into the earth. They can swim in seas. They can sparkle in light.

Fairies change their size and shape at will. They can be smaller than your thumb, taller than a giant Redwood tree, or everything in between. They can be quite beautiful or quite ugly. They appear the way they want to be seen.

Fairies can be good or bad. Good fairies help people in need. They make rainbows and flowers. They change the colors of the leaves in the fall. They weave magic into herbs to increase their healing powers.

Bad fairies kidnap women and carry off children to fairyland. They keep them hidden from everyone.

Fairies live among humans. But humans cannot see them unless they want to be seen. Look inside caves. Check along the roots of forest trees. You may even find them in your garden. But be quick! They will disappear in the blink of an eye.

There are five elements—air, earth, water, fire, and space—that make up our world. Fairies live in any of these elements. They protect plants, care for animals, hide in the clouds, and guard bodies of water.

LIFE CYCLE OF A FAIRY

Fairies go through many changes as they grow. They can live forever.

FAIRY EGG
A fairy lays one or two eggs on a leaf or a twig. The eggs are like tiny butterfly eggs and are covered in beautiful patterns.

FLUTTERPILLAR
After a few weeks, a flutterpillar hatches from the egg. The fairy mother feeds her newborn with milk.

COCOON

After many months, the flutterpillar's parents make a cocoon out of leaves, petals, or spider's silk. Then a winged fairy called a moppet emerges from the cocoon.

MOPPET

The moppet is still a baby and needs its parents' care until it grows fully at three years.

FAIRY FEATURES

BONES
A fairy's bones are hollow. They are filled with air pockets that look like a honeycomb.

COLLARBONE
A fairy has a fused collarbone like a bird. It is called a wishbone and helps her fly.

WINGS
Many fairies have four wings—two on each side. The wings reflect light, which makes them sparkle.

FEET
A fairy that lives on Earth has toes like humans. A fairy that lives in water has webbed feet.

EARS
Fairy ears are pointed.

MUSCLES
A fairy has lots of small, strong chest muscles that help move her wings. She has an extra set of flight muscles running down the middle of the back.

TYPES OF FAIRIES

Sprite fairies are small, supernatural beings. Some make their homes high in trees. Others live in water. Sprite fairies travel in swarms, and they can bite if you upset them.

SPRITE FAIRIES

Sylph fairies look like clouds. They help humans with their problems by helping them think clearly.

SYLPH FAIRY

NYMPH

Nymphs live among rivers, seas, trees, meadows, and mountains. They appear as young, beautiful, gentle girls. Nymphs are often honored for their creative powers.

Apsaras are a type of nymph. They are singers and dancers who perform at the courts of gods. They live in water, clouds, and the heavens. Because apsaras do not have wings, their wavy clothes help them fly.

APSARAS

GOBLINS

Goblins are evil, mischievous, and ugly fairies that live in caves and other dark places. They frighten children and make trouble. Goblins are always dangerous to human beings.

ELVES

Elves come from German mythology and English folklore. They appear as small nature spirits or beautiful young men and women. These friendly, kind fairies live in forests, under the ground, or in wells and springs.

Pixies are tiny fairies that rest under mushrooms. They fly with lovely butterfly or dragonfly wings, and some have blue or green skin. They nurture flowers and horses and can charm humans into joining their dances.

PIXY

Brownies are helpful fairies. They live in human homes where they do useful work. They like to keep homes clean every day.

BROWNIE

TOOTH FAIRY

When a baby tooth falls out, you put it under your pillow at bedtime and hope for a visit from a tooth fairy. A tooth fairy collects and uses the teeth to build her castle. In return, she leaves you a sweet gift.

Fairy godmothers have magical powers. They make good things happen to you as long as you believe in them.

FAIRY GODMOTHER

Fairies may not exist in real life. But they hold the promise of creating wonder and beauty for humans to enjoy.

Step outside and look closely at the nature surrounding you.
Perhaps a fairy will appear to cast magic and surprise you.

ABOUT THE AUTHOR

Suma Subramaniam is the contributing author of *The Hero Next Door*. She is also the author of *Centaurs*, *She Sang for India: How M.S. Subbulakshmi Used Her Voice for Change*, and *Namaste Is a Greeting*. She hires software professionals during the day and is a writer by night. Suma has an MFA in Creative Writing from Vermont College of Fine Arts and degrees in computer science and management. Visit her website at sumasubramaniam.com.

ABOUT THE ILLUSTRATOR

Martín Bustamante is an illustrator and painter from Argentina. At the age of three, he was able to draw a horse "starting by the tail," as his mother always says. As a teenager, he found new and fascinating worlds full of colors, shapes, and atmospheres in movies like *Star Wars* and books like *Prince Valiant*, by Harold Foster, that became his inspiration for drawing. He started working as a professional illustrator and has worked for several editorials and magazines, from Argentina to the United States to Europe.

GLOSSARY

being—a living thing

element—one of five substances (earth, water, fire, air, and space) that some people believe make up everything in nature

folklore—tales, sayings, and customs among a group of people

glimpse—a brief look

mischievous—able or tending to cause trouble in a playful way

mythical—based on stories from ancient times

supernatural—something that cannot be given an ordinary explanation

CRITICAL THINKING QUESTIONS

1. Based on what you've read, do you think most fairies are good or bad? Explain your answer.

2. Review the various types of fairies on pages 18–25. Which type of fairy would you most like to meet? Why? Which would you least like to meet?

3. Fairies can decide how they want to appear. If you were a fairy, how would you appear? Write a paragraph and draw a picture.

READ MORE

Hawkins, Emily. *A Natural History of Fairies: From the Notebook of Professor Elsie Arbour.* London, UK: Frances Lincoln Children's Books, 2020.

Sautter, Aaron. *Discover Gnomes, Halflings, and Other Wondrous Fantasy Beings.* Mankato, MN: Capstone, 2018.

Troupe, Thomas Kingsley. *Fairies.* Minneapolis: Bellwether Media, 2021.

INTERNET SITES

Fairy Facts for Kids
kids.kiddle.co/Fairy

Fun with Fairies
tscpl.org/books-movies-music/fun-with-fairies

READ THEM ALL!

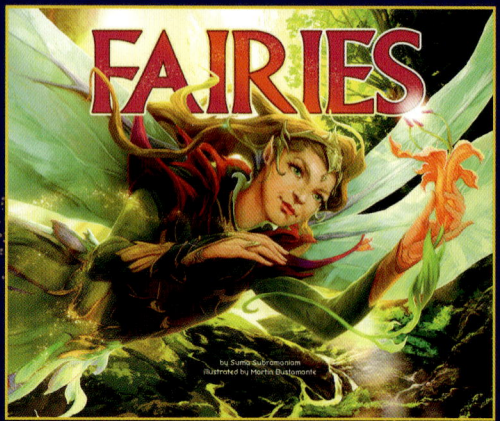
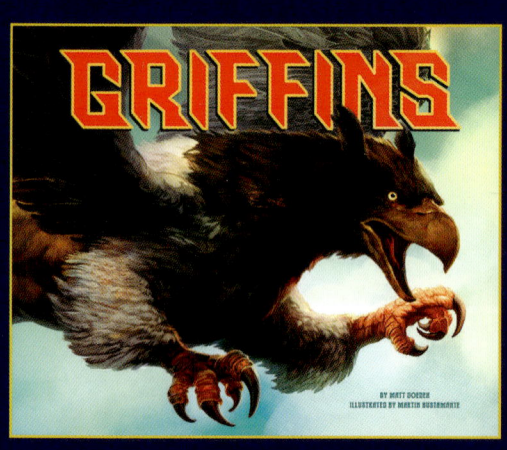
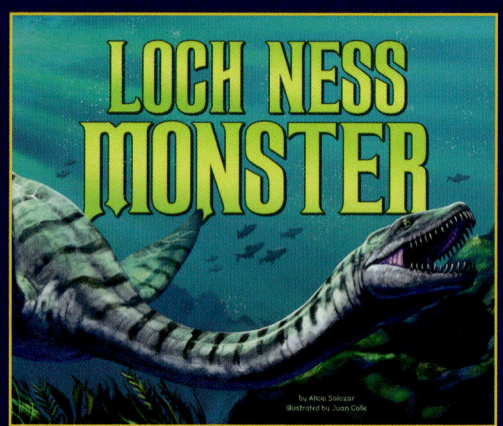
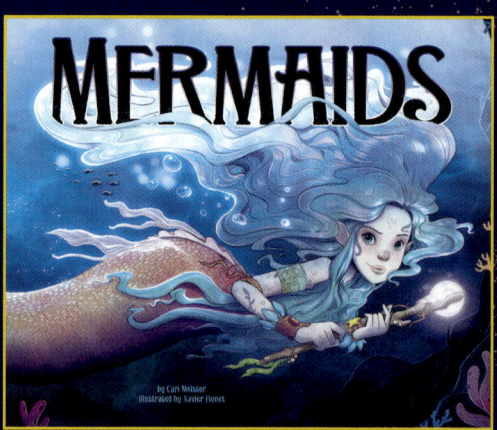